This Journal Belongs to

Published by

Real Joy Publications

Made in the USA
Middletown, DE
08 January 2022

58180749R00064